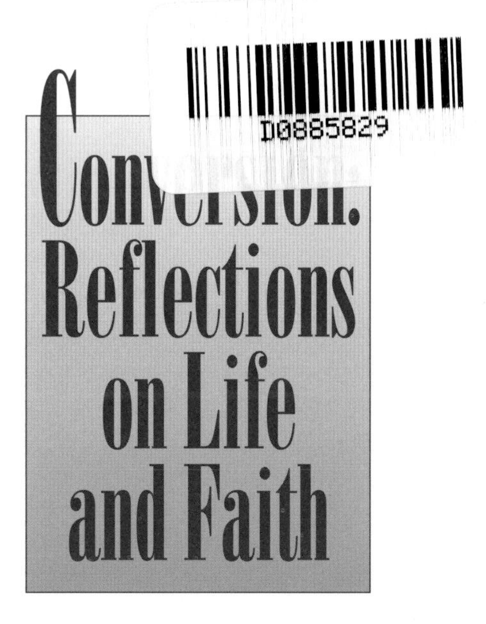

Conversion: Reflections on Life and Faith

JAMES TURRO

Allen, TX

NIHIL OBSTAT
Rev. Glenn D. Gardner, J.C.D.
Censor Liborum

IMPRIMATUR
† Most Rev. Charles V. Grahmann
Bishop of Dallas

October 29, 1993

ACKNOWLEDGMENTS
Unless otherwise noted, Scripture quotations are taken from or adapted from Today's English Version text. Copyright © American Bible Society 1966, 1971, 1976. Used by permission.

Excerpts from the English translation of *The Roman Missal* © 1973, International Committee on English in the Liturgy, Inc. (ICEL).

PHOTOS
Philip Coblentz (Cover)
Jean-Claude Lejeune vi–1, 42–43, 84–85

DESIGN
Davidson Design

Send all inquiries to:
Tabor Publishing
200 East Bethany Drive
Allen, Texas 75002–3804

Printed in the United States of America

ISBN 0–7829–0401–7

1 2 3 4 5 97 96 95 94 93

Contents

SERVING

Introduction

❦ I ride forever seeking after God . . .
For in my soul one hope forever sings
That at the next white corner of a road
My eyes look at him.

G. K. Chesterton

It has been observed, long since,
that we live in a mobile society.
But in all our coming and going
there is one journey that matters most,
the same one Elijah made—
the journey toward God.

God fortifies everyone for that journey,
as God did Elijah.
To us God provides word as sustenance.
These reflections, in the large,
ponder that word of God
so as to catch its flow
and draw off its strength.

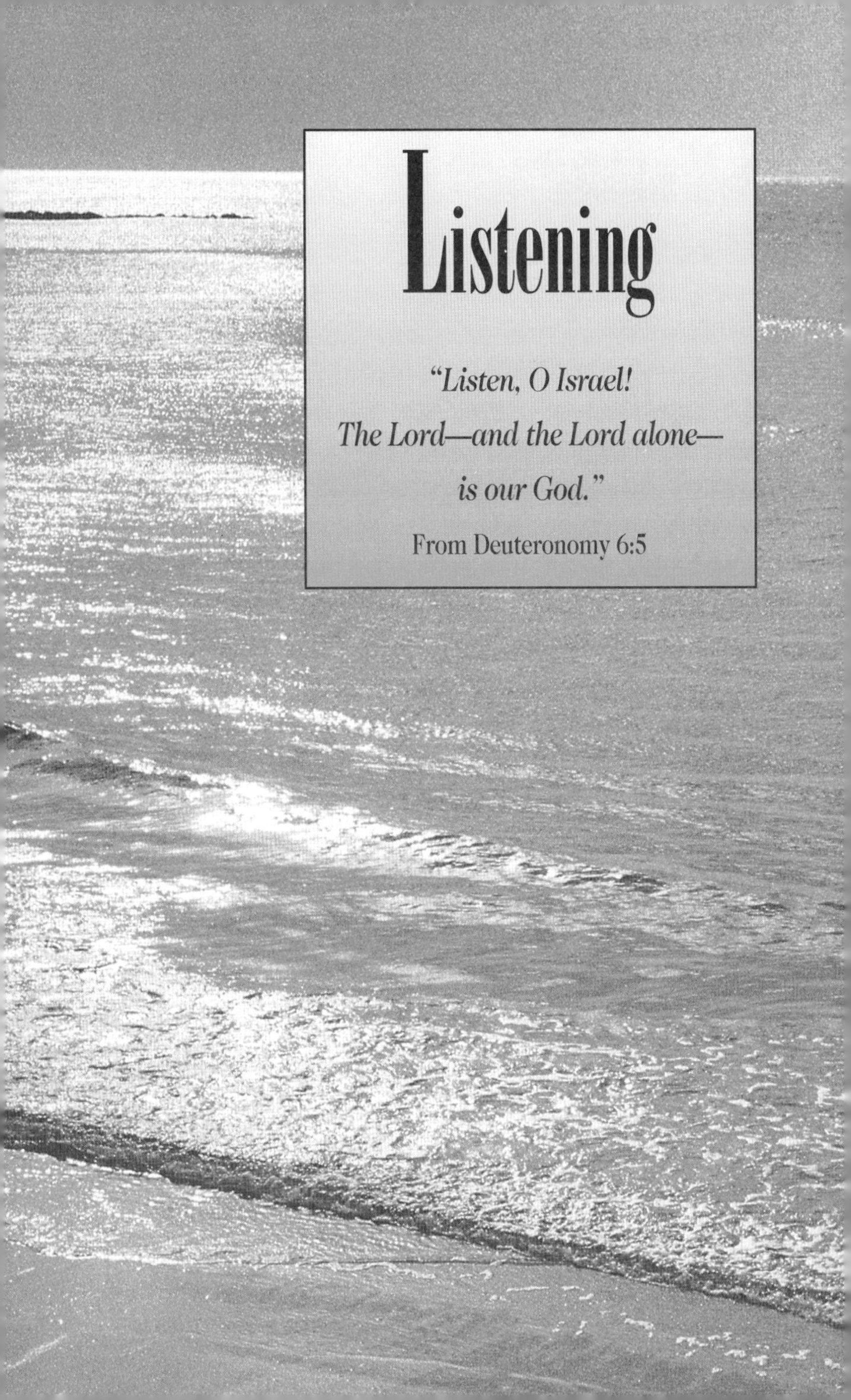
Listening
"Listen, O Israel!
The Lord—and the Lord alone—
is our God."
From Deuteronomy 6:5

"What Are You Looking For?"

Our Lord's first recorded words,
according to the Fourth Gospel,
came in the form of a question:
"What are you looking for?"
John 1:37

When Andrew and his companion
gave back their answer,
Christ went on to say,
"Come and see."
John 1:39

Over and over again,
as time unravels,
Christ keeps asking that same question:
"What are you looking for?"
and keeps offering the same invitation:
"Come and see."

In our work for the church,
we have been challenging people
to give thought to
the direction of their lives.
We have been inviting them
to think about the meaning
that they seek in life.

We have suggested that their quest
can be satisfied
only if they come to Christ
and stay with him.
In other words,
we have been keeping those compelling
first words of Christ alive
and resonating in our world:
"What are you looking for?"
"Come and see."

John 1:37, 39

A Song unto the Lord

A person is a song that God sings.
Each one of us is God's song,
God's way of softening and beautifying
life here on earth.
Let the world hear
loud and strong
that splendid melody
that God is humming—
the melody that is you.

A Harrowing Slump

In 1940 the top problems in public schools,
as identified by teachers, were
- talking out of turn,
- chewing gum,
- making noise,
- running in the halls, and
- littering.

In 1990 the teachers named
- drug abuse,
- pregnancy,
- suicide,
- rape,
- robbery, and
- assault.

By comparing these two lists,
one can measure the harrowing slump
that has taken place in American life.
There are good grounds for venturing to say
that in 1940 religion was more of a factor
in American life than it is today.

Youth of the past were better instructed
both in faith and morals
than they are today.
Is there a connection between
this fact and the lists cited above?
It would seem so!

Imaging God

At an airport terminal,
a man was seen wearing a T-shirt that
had these words printed on it:
What a friend we have in Jesus.
Below that line were written the words:
JONESTOWN—WACO.

Christians must find that
very offensive,
blasphemous,
cynical, and sad.
Sad because the words make us realize
that people form
their impressions of God
from the attitudes and behavior
of God's would-be disciples—
even when that behavior
and those attitudes are
as bizarre and insane
as were those of David Koresh.

It is sobering to think that
the picture of God
that some people have
is the picture of God
that you and I have painted
with our lives and our actions.

By the way that we have lived our lives,
we have represented
or misrepresented
God to people.

What an unspeakably grave duty we have—
never to give a distorted
impression of God
by what we do
or what we say.

God Be with You

I am in everything as a thread
through a string of pearls.
This is the achingly beautiful truth about God—
that you can meet God at every turn in life.
God is present
in the person who sits next to you right now,
in the breathtaking sunset you will see
across the hills tomorrow afternoon,
and no less in your daily tasks.
In all of these
there will be something of God
lurking, waiting to be discovered by you.

Catching a Glimpse—of God

Mary sits and contemplates Jesus
and she is praised for doing so.
We, too, are expected
to contemplate God—

- to consider the world in all
  its intricate parts,
  its utterly regular and predictable functions;
- to look on its morning fresh beauty,
  the breathtaking majesty
  of a redwood, for instance;
- to see in all this
  the power and greatness of the Creator.

It is said that we cannot see God,
face-to-face.
And that is true.
But we can catch a glimpse
of the hem of God's garment, so to speak,
in the splendor and magnitude
of God's creation.

Remembering the Giver

On the rim of a gold cup
that has come down to us from the sixteenth century,
one can read these few Latin words:
non donum sed donatorem,
"not the gift but the giver."
Every time the owner of that cup
filled it with rich aromatic wine
and brought it to his lips,
he was reminded by the words on the rim
of God's overflowing generosity and of the need
to acknowledge that generosity.

God, out of love, has showered us
with an abundance of good things.
And we have the tendency to fix on those things,
the material blessings
we have been given and
the success we enjoy,
forgetful of the Giver of all this bounty,
who is God.

What religion seeks to do
is to turn things around
and have us focus on the Giver
and not be distracted by the gift.

Pressed Down and Shaken Together

Once in a faraway country,
there was a kindly old man
who earned his living selling peanuts
from a pushcart by the side of the road.
One day, a little boy came by
and saw the tempting nuts
the man was selling.
The child's eyes filled with longing
but he had no money.

The good man, surmising as much,
told the boy to hold out his hands.
The boy made no move
but looked away shyly.
The man reached down,
took hold of the boy's hands,
cupped them, and
proceeded to fill them with nuts.
As the boy walked away,
munching on the peanuts
and smiling with delight,
someone who had witnessed the scene
asked the little boy,
"Why didn't you hold out your hands
when the man asked you to?"
The little boy replied, "His hands
are so much bigger than mine."

The boy, you see, was afraid
that his small hands could not contain
the generous helping the man would
put into them.

We realize that God's hands
are bigger than ours, and
the goodness God hands down to us,
we can scarcely contain.
God's goodness is a lavish goodness
that God has described as
pressed down,
shaken together, and
spilling over.

All Creation Praises God

The good things
that God has crowded in all around us
are marks of God's love for us.
A poet once said all this in a few marvelous lines:
His tenderness is in the grass of Spring.
His beauty is in the flowers.
His living love is in the sun above.
All here, and near, and ours.
(Source Unknown)

Close Encounter

When Moses went down from Mount Sinai
carrying the Ten Commandments,
his face was shining
because he had been speaking with the LORD;
but he did not know it.
Aaron and all the people looked at Moses
and saw that his face was shining,
and they were afraid to go near him.

Exodus 34:29–30

One cannot stand close to God
and walk away unscathed,
as Moses and the Israelites were to discover.
As an active Christian, you have had
some close encounters with God:
in prayer you have conversed with God,
in liturgy you have drawn near to worship God,
in lectures God's truth and God's will
have been declared to you.

All this has left its mark on you—for the better.
There is a better, brighter side
of your story than that which emerges each time
you examine your conscience
and come to confession.

We Are . . . as God Made Us

Self-acceptance is perhaps the fullest,
deepest surrender to God's will
that you and I can make:
to live peaceably and happily
with ourselves as we truly are, as God made us.
This is to embrace God's will for us
as Mary embraced God's will for her:
*"I am the Lord's servant. May it
happen to me as you have said."*
Luke 1:38

Yet it will not always be easy
to accept ourselves as we are.
There will come those dark moments
of self-doubt when thoughts
of our weakness and our inadequacy
will crowd in on us,
when we will become painfully aware
that others are what we are not
and others have what we do not.

For such bleak moments,
let me suggest this simple prayer:
O God,
if life is so many things
that I am not,
then give me the strength
to be what I am.

The Doorway of Ordinary Things

Stop to think of it.
Some of the most beautiful experiences
that we have in life come to us
through quite ordinary things:

- The flight of birds against a cloudless sky.
  How thrilling that can be!
  But those birds are only feather and bone
  and very common flesh.
- The piled-up, dark magnificence of storm clouds.
  How awesome that can be!
  But clouds are only so much
  accumulated moisture.
- A single seashell.
  How breathtaking that can be!
  But a seashell, for all its charm and neat design,
  is only lime.

The sharpest, deepest experience of God
that we can have in this life is like that—
it comes to us in a very ordinary way.
The elements of the Eucharist
are awfully commonplace—
bread and wine.
Yet through them
the greatness and goodness of God
enters into our lives and takes from us
some of the heaviness of living.

Promised to the Sea! Promised to God!

At some time or other
you may have stood and watched a river;
as you looked, you saw it turn and twist
through the countryside.
Then you saw it run straight as an arrow
through fresh meadows.
You saw it rush madly over jagged rocks,
then go quietly and gently on its way.
But always, always, fast or slow,
it was moving toward the sea.
A river is promised to the sea.
This is a picture of life.
As the river moves unstoppably toward the sea,
so we move through life toward God.
We are promised to God.
God could say to us:
As the river is promised to the sea,
so you are promised to me.

God with Us

A loving presence
cheers and encourages us.
It makes us feel strong and confident.
It makes us secure.
It is a sheer joy.

Let the Sun Shine In

Sunlight comes to a window,
and the same light comes
to a steel door.
But what a hugely different result
the sunlight has in each of these places.
The door blocks the light
and the whole inside of the building
remains cold and unchanged.
The window, on the other hand,
admits the sun
and the whole inside
is made warm and bright.

Saints—
and for that matter,
committed Christians—
are like the window.
They allow the light of Christ—
his truth and grace—
to enter into their little world,
to cheer and enliven it.

Two Words

One particular phrase keeps surfacing
in the accounts of our Lord's coming.
It occurs, in all, four times.

We first hear it
when John the Baptist is announced.
We hear it again in the Annunciation to Mary.
We hear it a third time in Joseph's dream.
And, finally, it is spoken
to the shepherds in the fields.

That simple phrase that so dominates
the story of Christ's coming
is just two words:
"Fear not."

How reassuring those words are to us—
who are prey
to all sorts of fears and anxieties in life;
who are inclined, for one reason or another,
to face every beginning with some trepidation,
fearful of what may lie in store for us.

But there is no cause to fear,
because Christ has come to earth
to be our Immanuel—
God with us—
to guide and protect us.
Therefore, *fear not!*

Golden Opportunities

The Arabs have a curious legend.
The legend tells how one day
a camel caravan arrived at an oasis.
The caravanners found a note pinned to a palm tree.
The note read:

> Pick up some pebbles
> and put them into your pockets.
> Travel a day's journey
> and look at the pebbles.
> You will be both glad and sad.

The travelers did just that.
The next day, as they took
the pebbles out of their pockets,
they found that the pebbles
had turned into nuggets of gold.
And now the travelers were glad and sad.
Glad that they had picked up a few pebbles,
sad that they hadn't picked up many more.

The year that lies ahead of you
will be strewn with pebbles for you,
pebbles of opportunity—
opportunities for honoring God and serving others.
Pick up as many as you can; they are pure gold.
And next year, at this time,
you will be very glad and much less sad.

Our Father Provides

One day, a little boy
stood waving a smudgy red flag
at the side of a railroad track.
Off in the distance
a freight engine and a single caboose
were approaching slowly down the track.
A man who stood watching all this
was prompted to walk over and say to the boy,
"You don't think that train is going to stop for you
just because you're waving that flag, do you?"
Then he added cynically, "Don't waste your time."

The little boy made no answer
but kept on studiously waving the flag.
As the man looked on, to his utter amazement,
he saw the train slow down
and finally come to a stop, just in front of the boy.
The boy put the flag down
and scrambled up the side of the engine into the cab.
As he reached the top,
the boy looked back at the man and said,
with a knowing smile, "The engineer is my father."

Sometimes, people chide us
for praying to God as we do.
They say, as the man said to the little boy,
"Don't waste your time."
But they forget that God is our Father.

Life—Flowing like a River

A river cannot run deep
until it finds its banks.
And so it is on the human plane.
Until we confront our limitations before God,
we cannot be profound.
This is not easy to do.
To admit that one has only a modest IQ,
no gift for words,
no power of observation,
no commanding presence . . .
this is hard to do.
Yet, hard as it is,
this moment of self-knowledge
must precede any success we hope to have in life.

It does make sense
to face our shortcomings,
to pray over them, and,
with God's help, to work within them.
It is then that we can hope
to achieve,
to succeed.
Otherwise we are like a stream
that ranges widely over the meadow;
it is a marsh,
a swamp,
but not a deep, fast-running river.

Esteemed as the Potter's Clay

For a moment,
picture an ugly glob of pigment
hanging from the end of Michelangelo's brush—
a brush made of hog bristles, at that.
Now watch as Michelangelo
takes and applies that pigment to a canvas
and, with objects that are altogether common,
a cheap brush and ordinary paint,
he begins to create a glowing masterpiece.

Sometimes, when we take a close look
at ourselves,
we become greatly disheartened.
We see ourselves as little more than
a tangle of faults and weaknesses,
a mess, born to lose.
But this is to forget that God can take us,
imperfect and blemished as we are,
and transform us
into a beautiful person—
just as an artist working with the vilest materials
produces a ravishing masterpiece.

God—No Less

"I made it to the top of the ladder
and found that the ladder was resting
on the wrong wall."
A man was once heard to say that
with much bitterness about his life.
What he meant, of course,
was that he had gone out after
the wrong things in life, pursued the wrong goals,
and realized it all too late.
His life was misdirected.

We must often remind ourselves
that the main goal in life that can alone
make sense for us is God—no less.
By all means,
want to have a good job,
want to make a good marriage,
want to raise a good family.
But above and beyond these things,
want to love and serve God,
want to do God's will
every day of your life,
want to be guided in your decisions
by the Spirit.

In other words,
rest the ladder of your hopes on God.

Then the day will never come
when you will have to say of your life:
"I made it to the top of the ladder
and found that the ladder was resting
on the wrong wall."

The Sufferings of Christ . . . in Us

If you should ever look closely
at a concert violinist
coming off the stage after a performance,
you would notice a kind of bruise
on the left side of the violinist's jaw.
This bruise is caused
by the rubbing of the instrument
against the violinist's neck as the violinist plays.

The ugly spot on the jaw
testifies to all the physical pain
and the mental anguish
it costs that concert violinist
to make the splendid music
that keeps audiences spellbound.

Good and great things can sometimes
come only out of suffering.
This was resoundingly true
of the Passion of Christ

Here I Am, Lord!

There is a religious order
that has a rather quaint fashion
of awakening to each new day.
Instead of ringing a rising bell or a buzzer
as was customary in most religious communities,
a prefect makes his way down the corridor,
tapping on each door as he goes, and saying,
"Wake up, Brother,
the Lord is calling you."

This is a fact not only in the life of religious novices
but in our own lives as well—
the Lord is calling us.
Each New Year's Day,
each Monday,
indeed on the morning of each new day of our lives,
Christ is summoning us to arise and embrace
a whole set of fresh opportunities
that beckon us to bring
the love and warmth of Christ to people
all around us who are hurting:

- people who are homeless,
  now found in ever increasing numbers,
- people who are away from home
  and are lonely,
- people who are widowed or aging,

- people who have experienced
  separation or divorce,
- people who suffer
  from physical or psychological illness.

Christ calls you to go out to all of these people—
and more!

Listen to Me If You Are Wise

The fact of pain and suffering in the world
is a deep, unbending mystery.
Have you ever thought that you
may have a part to play in that mystery?

There once was a man who was so deeply moved
by the suffering and pain he saw in the world
that he began to argue with God about it.
He challenged God, saying,
"Do you see all this hurt and grief?
What are you doing about it?"
And God answered,
"I have done something about it.
I made you."

Staying Afloat during Life's Storms

One day, two ships lay at anchor
in a quiet South Pacific harbor.
Suddenly, as often happens in that part of the world,
a ferocious tropical storm blew in from the open sea
and began to churn up the waters quite horribly.
The captain of one of the ships made a quick decision:
He pulled up anchor and sailed straight out
into the teeth of the storm.
The second ship stayed behind
in the relative shelter of the harbor.
Some days later, the first ship
came limping back to port,
very badly bruised but still afloat.
The second ship,
the one that stayed behind for fear of the storm,
had been washed ashore
and been severely shattered—beyond all repair.
How often in life this lesson
has been brought home to us.
The best way to overcome
our fears and anxieties is to go out
and openly and bravely confront them.
We can conquer even our worst fear in this way,
because God is with us.
Remember the words of Saint Paul:
I have the strength to face all conditions
by the power that Christ gives me.

Philippians 4:13

A Glimpse of the Splendor of God

One day, Moses asked to see the splendor of God.
And God granted this wish.
God agreed to disclose a little bit
of the greatness of God to Moses.
God had Moses station himself in the cleft of a rock
and God passed before Moses, proclaiming:
"I, the Lord, am a God
who is full of compassion and pity,
who is not easily angered and
who shows great love and faithfulness.
I keep my promise for thousands of generations
and forgive evil and sin."

Exodus 34:6–7

So many good things
may lie in store for us in the Christian life—
the security and joys of living in community,
the satisfaction of hard work,
the peace and serenity of prayer.

Best of all, we too will catch
a fleeting glimpse of God, and, like Moses,
we shall come to know that the Lord God
is full of compassion and pity,
is not easily angered,
shows great love and faithfulness,
keeps promises for thousands of generations,
and forgives evil and sin.

This Side of God

Perhaps you had the good fortune
of seeing the film *Sophie's Choice.*
It was an outstanding movie.
Sophie is a young mother
who lives in Eastern Europe during World War II.
At one point in the film,
Sophie and her two children, a boy and a little girl,
are arrested and carted off to a concentration camp.

Upon their arrival there,
one of the camp officials proceeds to tell Sophie
that, as a special favor,
she will be permitted to choose one of her children
to stay with her.
The other child must be taken away—
presumably to be killed.
Sophie cannot believe what she is hearing.
She cries out imploringly,
"Please! Please! Do not make me choose!"

But the camp official is adamant.
Either she chooses one of the children,
or both of them will be taken away and killed.
Finally, in a moment of exquisite agony,
Sophie manages to choke out the words:
"Take my daughter."

I can still hear the terrified screams
as the little girl is snatched up
and whisked away.
It was, I must say,
one of the most powerful moments
I have ever experienced in a theater.

What is it that creates
the monumental horror of that scene?
The simple fact that human life is at stake—
human life, the most precious and
most beautiful reality there is . . .
this side of God.

I Know Your Goodness

The future is full of uncertainty and surprise.
Yet there is one thing that *is* fast and sure
for the coming year—and for the entire future—
and that is the fact that God is good.
That is forever certain
and beyond all doubt and ambiguity.
God's goodness and kindness
will surely follow us
through all the days of our life.

The Glory of God

As you know, the rays of the sun,
which travel millions of miles
to reach earth,
never become detached from their source,
the sun's disc.
They are the sun's down-reach
into our lives.
They make us feel
the sun's warmth on our faces.

When God sent the Son to earth,
the Son of God did not become detached from God.
All of God's power,
all of God's goodness,
God's whole reality
continues to be in Christ,
who came to earth.
God lives in Christ,
as the sun lives in the beams it sends out.

God has reached down to earth in Jesus Christ,
to warm and brighten the lives
of those who live here—
to be a joy and blessing for you.

Cana Thoughts

All your life
you have been wanting something.
At first, it was toys.
Then, it may have been good grades.
Later, a job that was fulfilling and paid well.
But, more than anything,
you wanted a person with whom
to share your life in a deep and loving way.

And now that person
is sitting next to you—
someone eager to step into your life
and be dear and close to you;
someone who will put a strong arm
around you and hug you
in difficult times;
someone to laugh with you
in lighter moments;
someone to cry for joy
in moments of great happiness.
That someone
is God's very special gift
to you this day.

Thank God for that gift;
love and treasure that gift
all the days of your life.

Why Have You Abandoned Me?

Sometimes we feel so very down and out
as if everybody, God included,
had forgotten us.
Indeed, others may have forgotten
and become uncaring toward us
but God—never!
There is a remarkable line in Scripture
to remind us of this heartwarming fact:
"I have written your name on the palms of my hands."

Isaiah 49:16

This makes us think of a person
who has tattooed our name
not on some seldom seen part of the anatomy—
say on the back of the neck,
the upper arm.
But no, our name has been put on
the palm of the person's hands
so that now every time
the person glances downward
the person sees our name and
is reminded of us and our needs.

"You Are Mine"

Belonging is one of the clearest joys
we can have in life.
To be connected to some person,
place, or thing—
this somehow gives us a special
strength and reassurance.
Note the satisfaction,
the outright pride,
that people take in their belonging relationships.
People delight in telling us
how they are connected
as someone's father, friend, or teacher.

The gospels speak often about belonging—
belonging to God in Christ.
We belong to God.
Of all the interconnections that we have in life,
this connection is surely the most productive.
This link we have with God
introduces meaning and deep security
into our otherwise fragile existence.
We can draw much courage from the fact
that God has said:
"I have called you by name.
You are mine."

Isaiah 43:1

What Has Christ Accomplished—Through You?

The flea climbed aboard the elephant
as the elephant started to cross the bridge.
When they reached the other side,
the flea said,
"We made that bridge shake, didn't we?"

Sometimes we are as outrageous as the flea—
when we arrogate full credit to ourselves
for our achievements,
forgetful that we owe so much to God
in what we succeed in doing.
With an ingenuous candor, Saint Paul says,
"I . . . speak only of what Christ
has done through me."
Romans15:18

It is God
who is the Mover and the Shaker
in our life and work.
And we do well to acknowledge that fact.

Like Gold in a Furnace

One day,
a woman who was fatally ill
was visited by a friend
who had come to console her.
The sick woman instead
reassured her friend, saying simply,
"I know I'm going to cross the Jordan River
but I'm not worried.
My father owns both sides of the river."

The Book of Wisdom
expresses the same fact
in more exalted language:
The souls of the virtuous
are in the hands of God,
no torment shall ever touch them.
In the eyes of the unwise,
they did appear to die . . .
but they are in peace.

Wisdom of Solomon 3:1–3
THE JERUSALEM BIBLE

"You Are Greater Than . . ."

Sometimes,
in moments of self-pity,
we think of ourselves as complete losers.
But that can't be true!
Remember,
even a stopped clock is right twice a day.
In other words,
no matter how bad things stand,
we always have something to offer.
But the question is this:
The gifts you have, why were they given to you?

The New Testament cries out
the answer to you from every page:
The gifts you have are meant
for the support and enhancement
of the people around you.

This is the way one must translate
that concise and beautiful saying of Jesus:
"Love one another."
John 13:34

"Why Are You So Frightened?"

Our life is sometimes like a match.
It needs to be rubbed against a rough surface
to make its usefulness and beauty explode into full view.
This is a way of suggesting
that the difficulties we rub up against in life
can have a good result.
For God can bring good out of evil.
Remember that, and remember too,
that God will never allow us
to be tried beyond our strength.
In other words, except for sin itself,
there is no evil in life,
be it ever so vast and ever so terrifying,
that can fully and finally overwhelm us.

A New Commandment

"We do not need more light but more warmth.
[People] die from the cold
and not from the darkness. It is the frost
that kills and not the night." (Unamuno)
Christians profoundly believe
that what this world needs is love.
More than it needs advanced technology,
more than it ever needs the light
of new ideas or new philosophies,
this world needs the love and warmth of Jesus Christ.

"Blessed Are They . . ."

Everyone knows of Galileo's experiments
with a feather and a stone
dropped from the top of the leaning tower of Pisa.
Scholars consider that these experiments
marked the beginning of modern science.

It is stunning to reflect:
The progress of science
would have been slower
if that tower had stood straight and tall.
As it is, the very fault of the tower—
its crookedness—
has contributed richly
to the enhancement of human life.

How often it happens that some flaw
in our own lives
serves in the same way.
An illness—
a setback of any sort
that at first blush could seem to be
an irredeemable tragedy—
turns out to be productive of very great good.

There is much meaning in that
old saw that runs:
God writes straight with crooked lines.

"Your Treasure Is . . ."

Once in the course of his travels,
the Greek hero Ulysses
was kidnapped while he slept.
When he awoke, Ulysses found himself
in a place he could not recognize.
As time wore on, Ulysses, in his loneliness,
began to feel an excruciating nostalgia
for his native place, the island of Ithaca.
So pitiful was his longing
that the gods were moved and sent
a messenger to touch his eyelids
and make him see—to his great surprise and joy—
that he was in Ithaca all the while.

The world is pining for God,
as fiercely as ever Ulysses pined
for his native land, Ithaca.
There is a restlessness in the human heart—
an uneasiness that can only be defined
as nostalgia for God.
And just as Ulysses was made to see
that he had been in his beloved Ithaca all along,
the world must be made to see
that God, who is the object of *its* desiring,
has been here all the while:
The Word became flesh and
. . . lived among us.

John 1:14

"The Person Who Sees Me . . ."

Some years ago, the chief
of a remote and primitive tribe in Africa
was asked about his people's notion of God.
This was the chief's reply:
"We know that at nighttime somebody goes by
in the trees out there but we never speak of it."
That was all they knew of God.
For them, God was a formless mystery,
deeply unknown like the wind
rustling in the trees in the dark of night.

How ghastly it would be,
if this were all that we could say of God.
Happily it is not.
For us, God is not a vague reality.
We know God
to have substance, shape, and personality.
Best of all, we know that God
has care and compassion for us.
All this we know because God came
down to earth in Jesus Christ.
And countless people living in Palestine at that time
saw God and heard God, touched God and loved God.

And so we need never speak of God
as being the wind rustling in the trees.
Instead, we say that the Word became flesh
and dwelt here among us.

The Meaning of the Present Time

Seen on a bumper sticker:
"Enjoy life.
This is not a dress rehearsal."

If that is a way of saying
"Make the most of this life
because it's all there is,"
believing Christians must dissent.
Luke's gospel reports that
Jesus, hanging on the cross,
said to the thief crucified and dying
alongside him,
"I promise you that today
you will be in Paradise with me."
Luke 23:43

These words of Christ
are not devoid of meaning.
They imply, beyond question,
an afterlife.
Christians would rewrite
that bumper sticker so as to read:
"Enjoy life, but remember
the best is yet to come!"

Serving

"I have set an example for you,
so that you will do
just what I have done for you...
How happy you will be
if you put it into practice."

John 13:15, 17

He Passed By

The story of Jesus
can be summarized in just three words:
He passed by!

He passed by—
and what a dynamic passing it was!
He passed by a blind man,
and the man began to see;
he passed by a paralytic,
and the paralytic got up and walked;
he passed by a woman of easy virtue,
and the woman became a saint;
he passed by me . . .
and I cannot tell you the difference
that passing has made in my life.

Are you passing through life
in the same way Jesus did,
doing good on all sides,
making people and places better
for your having been there?

When your story is being told,
will people be able to say of you—
as they did of Jesus,
even if in a smaller way—
that you passed by?

Beyond Appearances

Once in his aging years,
Don Bosco had to travel to Paris.
Arriving at the city,
he went directly to seek lodging
for the duration of his stay.
The person in charge of the house
where Don Bosco was to stay
was not at all impressed by this visitor.
All he saw was a travel-worn,
scruffy, nondescript cleric.
And so he showed the traveler
to a tiny, dismal room far up on the sixth floor,
right under the eaves.

Years later, when Don Bosco was canonized,
this man was heard to remark,
"If I had known he was a saint,
I would have treated him differently."
The man had made the same sad mistake
those people made that Saturday morning
in the Nazareth synagogue.
They could see in Jesus
only the carpenter. (Luke 4:16-30)
The man made the same mistake
made by the Stoic and Epicurean philosophers
in Athens who thought Paul was a ragpicker.
(Acts 17:18)

All these people let themselves
be blinded by appearances.

We ought never to consider
how a person looks,
how a person speaks,
how a person dresses.
We ought to look beyond all that
to see the Christ-likeness
that is in everyone we meet.

"Love One Another As I . . ."

One of the truly great joys in life
is the warm and throbbing presence
of someone who loves us.
Consider how much it means to us
to have someone who loves us
present to us in times of suffering.
It somehow eases the pain.
And in good times, the presence of a loved one
serves only to enlarge our happiness.

Go and Tell!

Sometimes news comes to us
that we are bound to carry further.

If you are told there is a fire in the building,
what you are being told
is that a terrible power has been unleashed
that can destroy all life around it.
And so by every compulsion of charity and right reason
you are bound to do something about that—
to do at least two things:
- you must warn everybody else in the building about the fire;
- you must yourself leave quickly.

The passion, death, and resurrection of Jesus
is that kind of news.
It is saying that a terrible force has been released—
a force that does not destroy life but begets it.

By our words, by our works, and by our lives
we must declare that fact.
We cannot be silent about it.
This is the very directive the disciples received
from the risen Christ:
"Go and tell my friends to go to Galilee,
and there they will see me."
From Matthew 28:10

Go and tell.

Work and Worship

In Europe,
churches have often been built
right in the heart of cities and towns.
As a result, when one comes out of
a church, one finds oneself
not in a serene churchyard
or on a quiet neighborhood street,
but rather in the thick and swirl
of everyday life
where people are buying and selling,
meeting one another and conversing.

This is the very thing
that the Gospel implies for us—
that there is a connection,
a sequence between praying and living.
Our sentiments
of love and respect for Christ
must find quick and natural expression
in our everyday life and work.

"If you love me,
you will keep my commandments."
John 15:10

Christ the Divine Assistance

I once read a poem that imagined a young man
in New Testament times who was invited
to a dinner at which Jesus would be present.

Remembering that Jesus had once told a parable
about taking the lowest place at table so that the
host might invite you to come higher,
the young man sat down at the end of the table.
As the meal progressed, the young man
kept expecting that at any moment
he would be summoned to the head of the table—
but no such thing happened.
Finally the young man saw the Lord
get up and come toward him.
And the young man thought: "This is it.
Jesus is going to invite me to come higher."

But no. Instead, Jesus came and sat beside him.
Perhaps you too have waited
for a call to greatness in life—a call that never came.
Or perhaps you looked for a call that would draw
you out of some tragic situation that engulfed you.
But in vain.
Perhaps you failed to notice that, instead,
Christ the Divine Assistance has come
to stand by you to make you safe and important
just where you now stand in life.

The Shrine of Service

In the courtyard of a Franciscan church
in mid-Manhattan, New York City,
there is a dark bronze statue
of Saint Francis of Assisi genuflecting in adoration.
Visitors to the church have formed the pious habit
of touching the knee of the statue
as they pass by and whisper
a quick prayer of petition.
With the passage of time this custom
has worn the knee of Saint Francis,
bright and shiny.
It glows.

Our lives should be like that statue
exposed to the needs and appeals
of God's people—at their mercy.
Hurting people will come often
to lay their urgent requests upon us
- for prayers,
- for counsel,
- for a gram of loving attention.

So be it.
Such impositions, if accepted,
will only make our lives shine
like the knee of Saint Francis.
Ours will be a life made beautiful
by service to God's people.

What Will They Say . . . about You?

It will sound strange to say this,
but it is nonetheless a fact:
The most significant thing
that can be said of Mary
is that she gave in.
She gave in to God.
Mary bent her will to God's will
in all that she said and did.
"I am the Lord's servant. May it
happen to me as you have said."
Luke 1:38

When they come to tell your story,
your storytellers may have some
remarkable things to say about you.
They may say you were
- a hard worker,
- an effective manager,
- a brilliant student,
- a loving parent.

But, by far,
the most important thing they could say
is that you reverenced God's will
in all you said and did—
that you gave in to God!

Declaring Ourselves

Would it make sense for an orchestra
to play its music silently?
Or for an artist
to paint pictures invisibly?
Certainly not!
And neither does it make sense
for a person
to be a disciple of Christ secretly.

We Christians have to declare ourselves
by what we say and do,
even if, at times,
we stir up resentment in some.

Too often, we are tempted to keep hidden
our commitment to Christ,
either for fear of becoming unpopular
or out of fear of involving ourselves
in controversy or some unpleasantness.
But recall the strong and astonishing words
of the Gospel:
"Do you suppose that I came to bring
peace to the world?
No, not peace, but division."

Luke 12:51

The Light of the World

Few things in olden times
could have been as fascinating
as the lamplighter making his rounds.
Every evening, as night began to fall,
the lamplighter would make his way
down the high street of the village;
and wherever he stopped,
he left behind a warm and cheery light—
a light that would guide
and reassure everyone
who came by after him.

It would be hard
to think of a better way
of describing Jesus' mission on earth.

For Jesus did just that
in his life,
in his death, and, above all,
in his resurrection.
He kindled a great light,
a light of hope,
which continues to encourage us
as we make our way through life.

Jesus Came and Touched Them

It happened one day that the disciples
were in deep shock
from a traumatic experience
they had just had.
Jesus approached them
and touched them.
Suddenly, they were reassured
and at ease once again. (Matthew 17:1–8)

For two thousand years one of the chief goals
and thrust of the church has been
to extend the reach of Christ
into the lives of people—
to touch them with the truth of Christ
and so to give their lives meaning,
to touch them with the love of Christ
and so to make them
self-assured and strong.

I believe that the whole story of the church—
its hopes,
its intents and purposes,
its contribution to human society—
all of it is suggested and summed up
in that one line from the Gospel:
Jesus came to them and touched them.

Matthew 17:7

Not as the World Lives

Saint Francis of Assisi did some unusual things:
Francis threw his arms around a leper
and proceeded to kiss the leper's sores.
Once, when he was tempted to sin,
Francis rolled around in a thorn bush
until the temptation abated.
Francis lived as a common vagrant,
going from place to place,
without a home of his own.

No wonder Francis of Assisi
is considered to be the one person
who is the most like Christ,
for Christ lived in the same fashion.
Think for a moment:
Jesus directed his followers
to pray for their enemies and
do good to those that persecuted them.
Jesus associated with those that others
judged to be the lower elements
of the population—
irreligious people and tax collectors.
Jesus made no defense when he
was arrested and unjustly accused.

People just did not do those things.

Neither Christ nor Francis
lived and acted in the way
that people of their time
lived and acted.
When viewed against the background
of the people of their day,
Jesus and Francis were different.
They simply did not fit in.

There is a strong and disturbing lesson for us
in all this:
If we are to follow Christ
with somewhat the same success
that Francis had, we cannot
soak up the values of our world;
we cannot, in every instance,
think and act
as the "normal, fashionable people"
of our world think and act.
The Beatitudes
make this painfully clear:
To want to live in every respect
as the world lives
and still remain a Christian is like
having a mouth full of breakfast cereal
and wanting to whistle at the same time.
It cannot be!

Whoever Wants to Live . . .

Would it be too shocking to say
that Christ's birth must be our death?
Yet, in a sense, that is true.
When Christ is born in our lives,
we must somehow die.

We must die to those misshapen values
that we once lived by.
We must die to the prejudices
that once governed our lives.
We must die to the callousness
that we once harbored toward
our neighbor's hurts and needs.
We must die to . . .

We must die in these little ways
so that we may live unto Christ
in a large way.
What else can our Lord have meant
when he said,
"For whoever wants to save
one's own life will lose it;
but whoever loses one's own life
for my sake will find it."
Matthew 16:25

Whose Are You?

The gospels do not ask the question:
Who are you?
But rather, and more significantly,
they ask the question: Whose are you?

The conviction seems to be
that everyone must belong somewhere,
to someone or to something.
No one can be unattached, uncommitted.
And so you give yourself—
to God or to Mammom,
to sin or to grace,
to life or to death.
There is no escaping these polarities in life.

Whose are you?
You will be quick to respond,
"I am of Christ."
But stop for a moment to reflect.
Do your your thoughts,
your words,
your day-to-day behavior,
confirm your commitment to Christ?
Or belie it?
In other words,
are you a disciple of Christ
in fact or in fancy?

"Your Eyes See"

By the way they live and act,
some people make others
think of a little terrier furiously chasing
after an eighteen wheeler trailer truck.
The question is:
What will that little terrier do
when it catches the eighteen wheeler?

There is a terrifying emptiness
in some people's lives—a pointlessness.
Thank God, we are spared such futility.
As the Scriptures encouragingly assure us:
. . . we wait for the blessed day we hope for
when the glory of our great God and Savior
Jesus Christ will appear.

Titus 2:13

To Leave One's Mark

The ideal in discipleship is
to leave one's prints everywhere
on the work one is assigned to do,
on the companions one associates with,
and above all,
on the lives and faith
of the people one serves.

Faithful Virgin

Many people came to believe in Jesus
while he lived on earth—
but very few stood by him.
One group left
when Jesus began to speak of giving
his flesh to eat and his blood to drink.
This was rather too strong for them
and, so we are told,
many drew back from him and
would not go about with him any longer.
Later, when Jesus was arrested
and brought to trial, we read
"the disciples left him and ran away."
Matthew 26:56

They were fearful of being implicated with Jesus.

But the gospels do show us one person
who stayed true to Christ to the bitter end,
Mary his mother.
Mary stood on Calvary beneath the cross—
ever faithful.

Mary's robust faithfulness to Christ
must be an example for us.
We must not allow anything or anyone
to shake our commitment to Christ.

All Things Work for Good

One day a huge crowd gathered to hear Paul.
It would be the first time Paul spoke in Athens, and
his hope must have been running high.
Athens, in those days,
set the pace and tone for the whole civilized world.
If Paul "scored" there,
Christianity would get off to a good strong start.

But it was not to happen that way!

Paul gave his talk all right but, at the conclusion,
all that some people could say was:
"What is this ragpicker trying to make out?"
Paul failed miserably—or so it seemed.

Yet, in God's good time,
thanks to Paul's ceaseless efforts, not only Athens
but also much of the Mediterranean world
came to accept Christ.
All this makes us see that
we must not be too quick to admit defeat
in our efforts to do good.
If we take the long view, that is,
if we exercise more patience and persistence,
as Paul certainly did, we would come to see that:
In all things God works for good
with those who love God.
From Romans 8:28

Joy in Christ's Presence

John's gospel
tells of a group of Greek-speaking Jews
who had come up to Jerusalem
for the feast of Passover.
Approaching Philip,
who must have spoken Greek as they did,
they said,
"Sir, we want to see Jesus"
John 12:21
People come to the seminary
or to the novitiate
with the same request in their hearts
if not on their lips.
Maybe those people should be warned:
When once a person has seen Jesus,
that person cannot be cured.

"Bear Much Fruit"

Prayer and work for God
is not so much an obligation,
much less an onus.
It is rather a favor and a privilege
for which we should be supremely grateful—
We thank you for counting us worthy
to stand in your presence and serve you.
(Eucharistic Prayer II)

Faithful Stewards

A thought appropriate to the beginning
of a new year:
"Much is required from those
to whom much is given"
Luke 12:48

Jesus once told a parable about a sower
who went out to sow seed.
Some seed fell along the path
and was trodden underfoot or else
was consumed by the birds of the air.
Other seed fell on rocky ground
and though it sprouted,
it soon withered for want of moisture.
Still other seed fell among thorns
and when it grew, it was choked by thorns.
Finally, some seed fell in good ground
and yielded a hundredfold.

We have fallen on good ground.
Think of it.
We have the true faith to enlighten us.
We have the church to encourage us.
We have the sacraments to strengthen us
with the very strength of God.

In the parable of the sower
only a scant quarter of the seed fell on good ground,

and that quarter had to compensate by its productivity
for the three quarters of the seed
that was not so fortunate.
So it is with us:
"Much is required from those
to whom much is given."
Luke 12:48

"How Much More, Then . . ."

One day a man took his little son fishing.
It was a glorious day for the boy.
Way on into adulthood he used to think of it
as the best day of his life.
But when his father died,
the man went paging through
his father's diary.
He came on this entry:
Took my son fishing—a wasted day.

What a sad difference of opinion.
One wonders if something like that happens
from time to time in our life with God.
We have tried earnestly to pray.
God deeply appreciates the effort
but we judge it was a waste of time.
Sometimes what we think of as a waste of time,
God judges to be a beautiful prayer.

The Caravan Goes On

The Arabs have a saying that runs:
"Dogs bark but the caravan moves on."

These words bespeak an attitude of mind
that we must make our own
as we go about our duties in the Christian life.
It is an attitude of strong,
unswerving determination,
the same attitude displayed
by Peter and Paul,
those good soldiers of Jesus Christ.

Almost certainly,
as we go about our work within the church,
we will be subjected to unjust criticism
from thoughtless persons—
criticism for doing only
what the church expects us to do.
We must cultivate strength of character
so as not to be deterred
by yapping dogs.

We serve Christ and the church,
and, though dogs may bark,
our caravan will move on.

"I Have Set an Example for You"

One day a man walked up to Katharine Hepburn
on a street in New York City
and said to her, very simply but very touchingly,
"Thank you for all the happiness
you have given us."

Picture the last day of your life.
Ranging before you is an immense crowd of people.
They are all the people
whose lives you touched
by your words and your work.
What do they have to say about
your impact on their lives?

Would any one of them be able
to come forward to say,
"Thank you for the example of faith
that you have given us.
It was a mighty strength to us"?

Would any one of them be able to say,
"Thank you for the warmth and beauty
that your love brought to our lives"?

Would any one of them be able to say,
"Thank you for all the happiness
you have given us"?

"Who Do You Say I Am?"

One day, a man came up to our Lord and asked,
"What is it that you would most want to say to me?"
Without hesitation Christ replied,
"Love the Lord your God with all your heart,
with all your soul, with all your mind,
and with all your strength. . . .
Love your neighbor as you love yourself."
Mark 12:28, 30–31

From that disarmingly simple reply
we can know so very much about Jesus.
We can know, for example,
the set of values Jesus lived by,
the priorities Jesus observed in life,
the deep meaning that Jesus saw in life.

In a word, we can know
for what and for whom Jesus lived.
"What is it that you would most want to say to me?"
That is a question that can be put to you
to elicit an answer that will disclose as much
about you as Christ's response did about him.
Suppose you could write a letter and address
every human being alive in the world today.
What is the one single thing that you would feel
compelled to say to each one of them?

If you had just one sentence
to speak to every human being,
what would it be?
Whatever the sentence would be,
one thing you may be sure of:
it would tell us everything about you—
what you fear, what you live and hope for,
who and what you are.

Happiness in Your Law

Every now and then we are tempted to chafe
under the demands of church law.
It all seems so stifling—
the church's inflexible position on abortion,
on the obligation of Sunday Mass—
so very confining, so very limiting.
Let us admit it openly.
The law we live under is just that—
limiting and confining—but in a beautiful way,
in the way that an elevator and a banister
are limiting and confining.
They close us in;
they deprive us of the freedom of falling to our ruin.

In that same way,
Christ and the church fence us in,
so that we may not fall,
so that we may rise steadily and securely to God.

"Whoever Sees You . . ."

Rembrandt had a fascinating way
of portraying Christ.
He sought to convey an idea
of what Christ was like
not so much from the expression
that he painted on the face of Christ
as from the expression
he put on the faces of the figures
surrounding Christ in the picture.
So, on a Rembrandt canvas,
one comes to understand
the majesty of Christ
and his compassion
by reading the faces of the people
who stand around him.
It is they who declare the truth of Christ.

You might say
that this is our role in life—
to be like the figures
surrounding Christ
in a Rembrandt painting.
People can have an insight
into what Christ is like
by observing our life and our behavior.
In our small way,
we radiate Christ's vast goodness.

"Where Are the Other Nine?"

In the Far East, there once lived
an intensely holy Muslim.
One day, this good man felt the urge to pray
and make a rather extraordinary request.
He asked God to grant him the favor of doing good
without ever coming to realize it.
God granted his petition;
but as God thought about it,
God decided to grant that favor
to every human being.
And so it has been to this day.

How many people there must be for whom you are
a blessing,
a gift,
a sheer joy.
How many people there must be
who delight in the
little conversations you have with them,
inquiries you make after their health,
smiles you flash, attention you give.

How many of these beneficiaries
of yours there must be,
you may never know.
People hardly ever tell you
how much you mean to them.

"See What You Can Earn . . ."

Many questions rise in our minds
for which the gospels give no answer.
One such question is:
What became of those people
who were graced
by one of Christ's miracles?
Did the blind man,
who regained his sight at Bethsaida,
subsequently use his newfound vision
to feed his lust?
Did the paralytic, who lived in Capernaum,
use the mobility Christ gave him
to walk into a life of crime?

We are not told.

We may not have received
as dramatic a healing
from the hand of God
as those persons did,
but we have received gifts and graces,
many and great.
That raises a question:
Have we capitalized
on the opportunities that these graces
have made possible for us?
Or have we squandered them?

Praise God

A little girl who used to like to go
to church with her mother
was once asked how she prayed to God.

"Well," she said,
"first I tell God a ghost story.
Then I say the alphabet.
And then I show God
what I have in my Minnie Mouse wallet."

This is how that little girl used to entertain
visitors to her home and
this is how she sought to entertain God.

All this may seem childish to some,
but it is, in fact,
a prayer of surpassing beauty—
in its way a perfect prayer,
selfless and
sharply focused on God,
as all prayer should be.

Have you ever thought of praying
for no better reason than just
to please and delight God?

Some Received and Believed in Him

One day, the world-renowned tenor Enrico Caruso
walked into a bank in New York City
and attempted to cash a check.
The alert bank teller, seeing the famous name
on the check, became suspicious.
And the more Caruso tried to convince
the teller that he, in fact, was Caruso,
the more convinced the teller became
that he was a fraud.

Then Caruso had an inspiration.
Stepping back from the window, Caruso put his hand
to his chest and launched into an operatic aria.
Unhesitatingly, the teller began to count out the cash.
This was Caruso; there was no doubt about it.

The point, of course, is that
deeds speak louder than words.
Throughout the Old Testament period,
in the words of patriarchs and prophets,
God had been declaring affection for God's people.
And then one day—the first Christmas—
God put the matter beyond all doubt.
It is this that Christians commemorate
at Christmas—the ultimate proof of God's affection
and love for us in that the Son of God took flesh
and dwelt among us. (John 1:14)

God's Ways . . . Our Ways

The laborers in the vineyard complained
because although they had worked all day,
from sunup to sunset, they received the same pay
as those who had worked a single hour.

The elder brother of the prodigal son
resented the elaborate celebration
that was mounted in honor of the prodigal son,
who had taken his father's money
and squandered it in loose living.

We cannot help siding with people,
such as the elder brother.
We feel they have a real grievance.
How often in the gospels do we find persons
who think as we do—and say so?
Then we read on and discover
that Christ disagrees with our way of thinking.
The laborers in the vineyard
and the elder son are just two examples.
This serves as a strong lesson,
a reminder that God's ways are not our ways
and God's thoughts are not our thoughts.
We find it difficult to fathom
God's actions toward us and God's decisions for us.
But one thing we can know
is that every move God makes is right and good.

Power Went Out from Him

No one met up with Christ and was the poorer for it.

- Some had their slate wiped clean—
  Christ forgave their sins.
- Some were relieved of their physical disability—
  Christ healed their paralysis.
- Some were disabused of their mistaken notions—
  Christ enlightened them by his teaching.

One way or another they came away better persons
than they had been before encountering Christ.

What of those persons
who will meet with you this coming week?
You cannot forgive their sins.
You cannot cure their illnesses.
But you can cheer them by your smile.
You can strengthen them
by expressing your interest in them.
It is within your power
to make them feel good about themselves.
You can make a difference for the better in their lives.

Children of God

One day, when Saint Teresa of Avila
was still just a little girl,
she came to know that when martyrs die,
they go straight to heaven.

Without a moment's hesitation,
she sought out her brother, Rodrigo,
who was not much older than she was.
The two of them set out for southern Spain,
which was then occupied by the Moors.
The Moors detested Christians,
and Teresa was hoping that she and Rodrigo
would be seized and be put to death on the spot.
And thus they would be sped to heaven.

What a darling picture they must have made—
the small boy and his little sister, hand-in-hand,
trudging along the high road
that led from Avila to Salamanca.
Fortunately, the two were spotted by their uncle
who was traveling that same road,
and he promptly conducted them home.
You may think what you wish
about this action of Teresa.
You may think that it was ill-considered. It was.
You may think that it was imprudent.
It was that—childish even.
But you must concede that beyond all that
it was the action of a child,
a person for whom God was real and important.
It was the action of someone who took God seriously.

All this prompts the questions:
Is God real and important for you?
Do you take God seriously?

"I Know Your Works"

One day, Saint Teresa of Avila
was approached by one of her sisters
who began to enthuse about the praying
that she had done that day.
It had been
so satisfying,
so refreshing,
so very good,
that Teresa decided to test
the fiber and rightness of that prayer.
In the kitchen there was a quantity of potatoes
waiting to be prepared for dinner.
Teresa suggested that the sister
go down to peel the potatoes.
Her reaction to this request would make clear
to Teresa and to the sister
the authenticity of her praying.

Do you catch the implication?
The genuineness and rightness of a prayer
can be gauged by its spillover into everyday life.
With prayer, as with everything else,
it is true that by its fruits you shall know it.
In other words,
you can know the success of your praying
by your willingness to peel potatoes
and do other good works.

"You Can Be Sure . . ."

It sometimes happens at the turn of the year
that we fall prey to depressing thoughts
about ourselves. We get to wondering
whether we are succeeding or failing.
We wonder about the meaning of our lives.
Consider this.
Shortly after construction began
on Notre Dame Cathedral in Paris,
a visitor to the works was walking around
what would be the subbasement of this church,
dedicated to Our Lady.
He noticed a stone mason hard at work on a statue.
The mason was chipping away earnestly
with such an intense care and concentration
that the visitor could not refrain
from saying in wonderment:
"Why are you taking such pains with that statue?
Once the cathedral is finished,
who is going to see it way down here?"
The sculptor looked up quietly and responded,
"Our Lady will see it."

The good news this suggests is:
God sees what you do as you strive to please God—
even when others miss it or when they undervalue it
or when they judge it as failure.
God sees it all
and will reward and love you for it.

"Do Whatever He Tells You"

We prize a person's last words very greatly
We seem to feel that such words are a testament,
the gathered wisdom of a lifetime.

Mary's last words as given in John's gospel are:
"Do whatever he tells you."
John 2:5

Mary was not only speaking
to the stewards at Cana
but to us as well.
These words written in John's gospel
come as Mary's legacy to us
as we strive here on earth
to grow into authentic disciples of Christ.

These words of Mary are words
of breathtaking force and dazzling simplicity.
They are words that urge utter obedience to Christ
as we hear Christ's voice
in the gospels and in the teachings of the church.

If there is anything like a formula for success
in life and in eternity,
it must be Mary's words:
"Do whatever he tells you."

"My Father Is Always Working . . ."

Perhaps the saddest sentence
in the entire New Testament
is that spoken by that wretched man
lying at the side of the pool at Bethesda.
He had been sick for thirty-eight years,
and when Jesus saw him lying there,
Jesus asked him,
"Do you want to get well?"
John 5:6
And the poor man had to answer:
"Sir, I don't have anyone here
to put me in the pool when the water is stirred up;
while I am trying to get in,
somebody else gets there first."
John 5:7
"I don't have anyone."
This was the man's desperate complaint.
But then Jesus entered his life and he was cured
and no longer did he need to say:
"I don't have anyone."

When a disciple of Christ is present,
no one in dire straits ever has to say,
"I don't have anyone."
The disciple is there to bring into that troubled life,
something of the love
and warmth
and compassion of Christ.

"I Am the Vine"

One day a missionary serving in Africa
was talking about Jesus—
about how loving and compassionate Jesus is.
An old African woman listening in the crowd called out:
"We know him. He was here once."
It turned out that she meant another missionary,
a very holy person,
who some years before had evangelized that region.
That former missionary's goodness
had been so intense
that this woman could confuse the missionary
with Jesus.
This suggests a beautiful fantasy—
to imagine that, sometime hence,
someone will be telling the story of Jesus to a little child.
And with the pardonable confusion of childhood,
that child would cry out:
"I know him. He was here once."

And all the while the child would be meaning you.
Is your goodness,
your religious spirit, such that
someone could—
by even the widest reach of the imagination—
mistake *you* for Jesus?

Walk as Children of the Light

On the occasion of a baptism
one looks at the infant's clenched little fist
and imagines the power and possibility
that is locked in that fist.
In the years to come that fist can open wide
to do some cunning things—

- caress his mother's face,
- give his father a solid handshake,
- reach out to grasp a wildflower,
- pet a puppy.

One day, too, that fist will open wide
to make the Sign of the Cross
to honor God.
And who knows but that someday
that fist
may clutch a surgeon's scalpel
and bring fresh life
to a dying person,
or it may stretch wide
to trace out a priestly absolution
that will restore grace and peace
to a troubled spirit.

It is the beginning
of such a bright future for this child
whom we are looking on today.

"Remember, then,
what you were taught
and what you heard."

Revelations 3:3

"Do This in Memory of Me"

Some things are too beautiful and too meaningful
ever to be forgotten.
The fact of Christ is one such thing.
The glamour of Christ's teaching,
the power of Christ's sacrifice
demand to be remembered.

It is not extravagant to say
that the task of the Christian
is to keep the memory of Christ alive—
to go out and reassert
with vigor and conviction
the teachings of Christ,
to renew his sacrifice.

Back in the first century,
a canny little man, Paul of Tarsus,
described the church's great memorial action,
the liturgy, in this way:
Every time you eat this bread
and drink from this cup,
you proclaim the Lord's death until he comes.
1 Corinthians 11:26
This is what the Christian must do—
proclaim the death and the life of Christ,
until he comes again.

Our Tomorrows Are Christ's Yesterdays

In the New East where Jesus lived,
contrary to the practice
in many other parts of the world,
the shepherd
often goes ahead of the flock,
not behind it.

Christ is our Good Shepherd.
He goes before us.

All through the bitter memories
that Holy Week evokes,
we take comfort in the thought
that Christ has gone before us
in any of the troubles
that we may have to face.
He will understand;
he will pity.
All our tomorrows are his yesterdays.

During the Easter Season, as we celebrate
Christ's resurrection and ascension,
we realize with joy
and immense relief
that once again Christ goes before us,
to anticipate an experience
that in time will come to us.

Once in Royal David's City

Birds are meant to fly.
They have wings;
they have just the right form and build to enable them to glide,
to soar,
to plummet.
Yet for all that,
no bird can leave the ground
unless it is given one more thing—
a current of air.
Birds cannot fly in a vacuum.

Just as birds are meant to fly,
we are meant to live forever in happiness.
We have a passionate desire for this,
a taste for it,
but of ourselves we can never bring it about.
To realize this longing,
we desperately need
a special assist from God.

Christmas is the celebration
of God's down-sweep into our world—
to give us just the lift we need
to realize our destiny.
The Word has been made flesh,
and now God is the air under our wings.

Transforming Ourselves into Christ

The German people make a delightful play on words.
They say: *Man ist was man isst*—
"a person is what he or she eats."

You and I eat the Body of Christ.
What must this say about us,
about who we are and how we act?
Have you ever stopped to think that
this may explain the love and goodness
that we find in ourselves?
It is the eucharistic food we eat taking effect in us;
it is something of Christ that has become part of us.

Conversely, have you ever stopped to think how
much weaker, meaner, sicker individuals
we would almost certainly be
if we did not sustain ourselves
with the Body of Christ, because:
Man ist was man isst—
"a person is what he or she eats."

One Blessing after Another

Christmas is the celebration of a loving presence.
The presence of God
came down to earth in Jesus Christ
so that God might be near us to support us
and to enliven our existence in a thousand ways.

Benjamin Disraeli once wrote these astonishing words:

> *Youth is a blunder;*
> *[adulthood] a struggle;*
> *old age a regret.*
>
> **Conings** [1844], Bk. III, Ch.1

How bleak, how dismal these sentiments are.
They express the hopelessness and meaninglessness
of life as some people experience it.

Part of the joy of Christmas is the fact
that Christ comes to rescue us from such a fate.
His coming has put meaning and purpose
into our lives:
The Word became flesh . . .
and lived among us. . . .
Out of the fullness of his grace he has blessed us all,
giving us one blessing after another.

John 1:14, 16

Thank God, we shall never have to say:
Our youth was a blunder;
our adulthood, a struggle;
and our old age, a regret.

Giving Thanks

There is an account of a hunter
in a remote part of Siberia
who lost his bearings in a deep forest.
Near dead from tiredness and exposure,
the hunter stumbled upon an empty cabin.
There he spent the night, and by morning
he was once again fresh and fully revived.
As the hunter left the hut
he left behind a small portion of rice,
some tea, a few matches,
and some firewood for the next wanderer
who might come by that way and need
warmth and sustenance.

What an exquisite way of saying thank you
for the rescue that had come to him,
to leave something behind that would be of help
to someone else in need—
someone the hunter would never
even see or come to know.

God has rescued us many times over,
as we have occasion to reflect upon
every Thanksgiving Day.
What a sensible and inspired way for us
to return thanks to God,
—as that gentle hunter did—
by an act of goodness and compassion for others.

Remember and Forget Not

Would it seem strange,
and perhaps even wrong, to say
that one of the most serious obligations
we have as Christians is: to remember.
There are stories in the Old Testament
in which God took the people to task
for their failures to do just that—
to remember.
God chastised the people
for their failure to remember
that God had led them out of Egypt,
for their failure to remember
all the other good things
God had done for their ancestors.

Ever mindful of this obligation,
the church does not let a single day
go by without remembering.
For that is precisely what liturgy is—
a solemn, loving remembrance
of Christ's death on Calvary.

"No Greater Love . . ."

On October 12, 1972, a Fairchild F227
took off from the airport of Montevideo, Uruguay,
for Santiago, Chile. It never arrived.

Somewhere in the upper reaches of the Andes
the plane crashed, plunging its crew and passengers
into one of those fierce and elemental experiences
that befall human beings from time to time.

For ten solid weeks, sixteen survivors struggled
to stay alive by munching on a few bars of chocolate
and drinking from a few bottles of wine that had
been brought along as occasional refreshment
for what they believed would be a short air trip
of a few hours duration.
But as the days dragged into weeks
their pathetically small supply
of food became exhausted
and a terrifying realization took hold of them.
If they were to survive, they would have to partake
of the only nourishment now available
to them in all that snowy waste:
the flesh of the dead bodies of their friends.

As it happened, most of the survivors
were young men, graduates of Catholic colleges,
who had enough theological sophistication
to understand that this course of action would be

entirely compatible with their Christian commitment.
And, yet, they could not master
the ferocious revulsion they felt
at the thought of consuming human flesh. Until,
that is, one of their number was inspired to say:
"We should do this.
It will be like Holy Communion.
When Christ died, he gave his body to us
so that we could have spiritual life.
My friend has given us his body
so that we can have physical life."

An insight into the Eucharist
that is as true as it is touching.

Mary Was That Mother Mild, Jesus Christ Her Little Child

When the Advent wreath is lighted
in some churches in England,
the fourth candle of the wreath
is lighted "to honor Mary,
the mother of Jesus and God's obedient servant."
This is precisely why the church
celebrates feasts in honor of Mary.

The beauty of Mary's life and
its vast importance for our salvation demands
no less than that—that we honor her as
the mother of Jesus and God's obedient servant.

A World with and without Christ

Every year at the Easter Vigil
on Holy Saturday night,
as we begin our Easter celebrations,
the church building is plunged into total darkness.
This is meant to be an ominous reminder
of how dark and bleak and loveless
this world is without Christ.
Then, at a certain point during the Easter Vigil,
a single lighted candle is introduced into the church.
This is to make us understand
the warmth and brilliance
that Christ brings into the world.

You must be that lighted candle.
You must make us experience, often and deeply,
the goodness, warmth, and compassion
of Christ in the world.
On Holy Saturday, when that single lighted candle
is brought into the darkened church,
we hear the simple words,
  Christ our Light;
and the people respond,
  Thanks be to God.

Your life and work must make the joyous statement:
  Here is Christ our Light.
And we shall be compelled to answer,
  Thanks be to God.

Of That Fullness We Have All Received

There is an ancient legend
about the death of Christ.
The legend describes how some drops
of Jesus' blood fell to the ground
as Jesus hung on the cross;
and wherever that blood landed,
there sprang up brilliant red flowers, anemones.

Surely you understand that this legend
is only an attempt to declare in a dramatic way
a great truth about Jesus' death.
And it is this:
The death of Jesus has had
enormously good and beautiful results for us all—
results that are like flowers,
which brighten our lives and make them joyous.
The death of Christ, like the life of Jesus,
was full of grace and truth,
and of that fullness we have all received.

(John 1:16–17)

"Do This . . ."

Just think for a moment of some of the
significant words that turn up in the gospels—

Come
Go
Follow
Serve
Give

You see immediately that these words
are all action words.
They call us to perform actions that will bring
honor to God and
benefit to our neighbor.

This is all a way of saying
that Christianity is not so much a religion of
learning or
believing or
feeling
as it is a religion of doing.

At every eucharistic liturgy,
we have a powerful reminder of this.
The priest elevates the chalice, having said,
Do this in memory of me.
We must not only do the Eucharist in Christ's memory;
we must do all the teachings of Christ.

Some Sixty . . . Some Thirty

At the first stirring of life,
a seed in the ground
shoots down a stem
into the earth beneath it.
This it does to steady itself
and to suck up nourishment
found in the rich soil.
Then, as a second step,
the seed sends up a sprout above ground.

This is a kind of analogy
of our own behavior
at the start of each week
when, on Sunday, we assist at liturgy.
Through prayer
we sink down roots into God
and draw strength and steadiness
from the Divine.

Supported in this way,
we put our head above ground,
prepared and fortified
for all that life may aim at us
in the oncoming week.

The Spirit of Life

Few things in life are
more depressing and deenergizing
than the memory of past failure or defeat.
Such a memory sits in our consciousness
like a dead weight
and keeps us from advancing.

Fortunately, our Lord
has addressed these worries.
"Come to me,
all of you who carry heavy loads,
and I will give you rest."
Matthew 11:28

This thought must rise to mind
each time we celebrate Pentecost—
a celebration of triumph.
Celebrating Pentecost makes one realize
that the Christian faith alone
can vanquish defeat
because it was born in defeat.
But the monumental defeat of Good Friday
gives way to the success and triumph
of Easter and Pentecost.

"When You Pray . . ."

Saint Ignatius once hired a porter
to carry his baggage on a journey
that he and his followers were taking.
On the trip,
from time to time,
Ignatius and his followers
would pause and pray.
This somehow fascinated the porter
and he conceived the wish to pray, too.
When he shared this desire with Ignatius,
the porter received an astonishing reply.
Ignatius told the porter
that he had already prayed—
that the desire to pray
was prayer itself.

Think of the times
you felt the desire to pray
more and better than you think you do.
The same must be said of you
as was said of the porter:
Your desire to pray more and better
was itself a prayer—
a hauntingly beautiful prayer in the sight of God.

A Mystery of the Greatest Magnitude

Mardi Gras,
which precedes Lent every year,
is really a Christian feast—
improbable as it may seem.
In its own grotesque way,
Mardi Gras celebrates the happy consequences
of the suffering, death,
and resurrection of Christ.
And so, for instance, the liberation that Christ
won for us by his death is expressed
in the free and relaxed spirit
of the Mardi Gras festivities.
The utter defeat of evil and evil forces
accomplished by Christ's death is expressed
in the bizarre devil masks and costumes
that are worn.
The devil, now, is not so much to be feared
as to be laughed at and made fun of—
as these whimsical masks and costumes suggest.

All of this is saying in a folkloric way
that the suffering, death,
and resurrection of Christ
is a mystery of the greatest magnitude—
the like of which is not to be found
elsewhere in history.

They Come to See . . . and Stay

When Philip told Nathanael that Jesus
was from Nazareth, Nathanael replied scornfully,
"Can anything good come from Nazareth?"

John 1:46

It was then that Philip said, *"Come and see."*
Well, Nathanael came and stayed
to believe mightily in Jesus.

November is the month of All Saints.
The saints can be thought of in just this way.
They are people who come to see if any good can
come out of Nazareth. When they find that it can—
and does, they, like Nathanael, stay
to believe and reverence Christ to the full.

This is the blazing example for us.
We, too, like Nathanael and the other saints,
must take Christ seriously. We must come to
discover that great good, indeed the greatest good
of all, comes from Nazareth—and it is Jesus Christ.

Death Has Lost Its Sting

If the believing Christian can manage
to face death with equanimity,
this should be no cause for surprise.
"We worship Someone who knows his way
back from the dead." (G. K. Chesterton)

"The Kingdom of Heaven Belongs to Them"

It has been remarked
that in times of turmoil
people are prone to ask,
"What is this world coming to?"
But, by far, the more rewarding question is not:
"What is this world coming to?"
but rather:
"What has come to this world?"

The gospels have a ready answer
to that second, more rewarding question:
The Word became flesh . . .
and lived among us.
John 1:14

It is God who has come to our world.
And the added good news:
When God came—comes—
God gives to those who believe
the power to become children of God.
Out of the fullness of God's grace
God has blessed us all,
giving us one blessing after another.
John 1:15

The Greatest Love

When Hoover Dam on the Colorado River
was dedicated in 1936,
note was taken of the human lives
that had been lost in the course of its construction.
An inscription was set in place, which read:
"For those who died [here]
that the desert might bloom."
During Lent, Christians reflect on a death.
But this is not as morbid as it may seem—
for we are thinking and praying
over the death of Jesus Christ,
a death that has made the desert of our lives bloom.

Through Him, with Him, in Him . . .

Sometime you must look carefully
at one of those pictures of Our Lady
that come from the Eastern Church.
Our Lady is always pictured
with the child Jesus in her arms,
and always her head is tilted toward the Holy Child.
This tilt of Mary's head is meant
as a gentle and quiet reminder that says:
This is Jesus, the center of my life and yours.
This is the meaning of our religious profession.
It is a declaration to the whole wide world that we
have taken Our Lady's cue to heart and, in fact,
have made Jesus the center of our life and work.

Baptized into His Death . . .

Tears may flow in the night,
but joy comes in the morning.

Psalm 30:5

These words define the life of Jesus on earth.
After the misery and desolation of Good Friday
came the resplendent joy of Easter morning.
It is our destiny to repeat in our lives
the experience of Christ.
Life on earth can too often be a Calvary for us,
but we know that Easter
will follow for us as it did for Christ.
Let us draw courage from this thought.

Our Rising to Life

A British artist once executed a vast painting
of Christ entering Jerusalem.
And as a model for Christ
the artist used his own face—
he painted himself into the picture.
During the Easter celebration,
this is precisely what the church
encourages us to do—
to paint ourselves into the picture,
to understand with peace and great joy
that as Christ rose from the dead
so indeed shall we.

"My Soul Is Glad . . ."

Someone has sagely remarked,
"I think only about the future;
after all, that is where I am going
to spend the rest of my life."
The church very much approves
of this line of thought.
The church wants us to think often
about the hereafter—
where we will spend
most of our existence.

This is one reason
that the church celebrates feasts,
such as the Assumption.
The Assumption celebrates
Mary's entry into the next life,
a life of unending happiness with God.

This is the same destiny
that awaits every one of us
who exits this life as Mary did—
in God's favor, that is.

"He Shall Be Called . . ."

Has it ever caught your attention,
how many names and titles
are given to Jesus Christ in the gospels?
He is spoken of as
Lamb of God,
Immanuel,
Lord,
King,
Good Shepherd,
and a whole array of other designations—
too numerous to mention here.

Why should this be?
It is because of the largeness of Christ.
No one word can encompass
the broad and deep reality that is Jesus Christ—
no one word can say all that must be said of him.

And even with that long list of names
that have been found for him,
we have not succeeded in capturing with our words
all the richness and abundance and beauty
that is Jesus the Christ.

"To Whom Shall We Go?"

If the Magi
had to go out and look for Christ on their own
without the guidance of the star,
where would they have looked?
Probably they would have searched him out
in some resplendent palace
on the banks of the Nile, in the proud city of Rome,
or in some gilded mansion in Athens
or some other great city.
But surely the Magi would not have come to Bethlehem
and peered into that miserable cave outside the town.
And yet it was just there in that unlikely spot
that Christ was to be found.

If today some unchurched person
should go out in quest of an experience of God,
where would that person go?
In all likelihood such a person would go

- to some mountaintop
  surrounded by a majestic forest
- or to the shores of a mighty ocean
  there to make contact with the power of God
- or to a book crowded with deep thoughts and
  brilliant ideas.

But the real, powerful experience of God
is not to be found in any of these places
but rather, in the small host that is the Eucharist.

Receive the Spirit's Flame

How vastly different you are today
from the way you were when you were two days old.
And this huge transformation of you
has taken place without your sensing it.
After all, you have not felt your hair growing nor
have you sensed your height and weight increasing.
You did not see these changes
as they were happening—
you did not hear them nor smell them.
Yet undeniably they have happened.

All this goes to show
that we cannot always use our senses
to measure reality.
Things do happen without our perceiving them.

When you first began to study about our faith,
you were told that the Holy Spirit
lives and acts within the church community.
You were told that when you received confirmation,
the Holy Spirit would come to you in a special way.
Very likely you did not sense the Spirit's coming
when you were confirmed.
The Holy Spirit does not arrive noisily.
Yet, it is true
that the Holy Spirit came to the church
on that first Pentecost

in a rather conspicuous,
even flamboyant manner. (Acts 2:1–3)
The Holy Spirit normally comes
in a less tumultuous fashion.
The Holy Spirit is working within the church,
within you and me,
quietly, subtly—but very, very definitely.

The Lord, the Giver of Life

One of the less cheery bumper stickers
seen about town declares:
Life is tough and then you die.

What a harsh and dismal way
to tell the human story:
a joyless life followed by never-ending death.
How different the message of Christmas.
It does not announce
that everlasting death awaits us.
Quite the contrary,
Christ speaks of his coming in this way:
"I have come in order that you might have life—
life in all its fullness."

John 10:10

Thanks Be to God

Once every year
we take time out to say thanks to God
for all God's goodness to us.
And that's just as it should be.
But better still as a "thank you"
would be to do something to express our gratitude.

There is a beautiful woman
who is mentioned just once in the gospels—
Peter's mother-in-law.
Jesus once cured her of a fever.
She immediately got up from her sick bed
and began to wait on Jesus and
the others who were with him.

Service to God and to human beings is unbeatable
as a way of expressing our thanks.
It is a strong and effective way,
a very beautiful way of saying thanks.

"All People Will Call Me Blessed"

Whenever we set ourselves to remembering
about great happenings,
invariably our minds go out to scientific breakthroughs.
We think of nuclear fission, for example,
or the conquest of outer space.
But the fact is that great things happen
on other levels of reality as well.

One remembers the coming together
of the human and divine—
the incarnation of God.
That great happening was like
the sky reaching down to touch the earth.
And when we think of that
explosive, great happening that it was,
we must think of the place where it happened.
Most improbably it came to pass
within the body of a plain, Jewish maiden,
Mary of Nazareth.
That explains the high importance
that Catholic Christians find in Mary—
Mary served as the place, the time,
the circumstance
of God's great coming to humanity.

"From now on all people will call me blessed,
because of the great things the Mighty God
has done for me." Luke 1:48–49

Reborn as God's Adopted Children

The cross on Calvary
casts a dark and ominous shadow.
The empty tomb on Easter Sunday
gives off a brilliant light.
During Lent, the church wants us to experience
both the shadow of the cross
and the joyous light of the resurrection.
The church does not want us to imagine
that we are mere bystanders
seated in the audience
watching with detachment a passion play
that is being performed on stage.
But rather, we—you and I—are caught up in the action.

Our destinies are profoundly involved
in the suffering and resurrection of Christ.
It is to drive home this conviction
that the church prescribes forty days of penance—
of fasting, abstinence, prayer, and almsgiving—
so that we can taste the bitter agony of the cross.
And this is why, too, that on Easter Sunday
the church celebrates with glad abandon—
so that we can feel deep down within us
the sheer joy of the resurrection,
Jesus' triumph over death.
This is the bittersweet mood of the Lenten Season.
But take careful note of this:

What begins in shadow, ends in light!
In other words, there is a happy ending
to the story of Christ and to our own story as well:
By suffering on the cross
he freed us from unending death,
and by rising from the dead he gave us eternal life.

Preface, Sundays in Ordinary Time II

Come, Let Us Worship

During Lent the church brings into sharp focus
the suffering and death of Christ.
Every painful detail is rehearsed:

- the agony in the garden,
- the brutal interrogations,
- the flogging,
- the crowning with thorns.

And then on the afternoon of Good Friday
the church solemnly unveils the crucifix
and confronts us once again with the full horror of it.
Surprisingly, the church does not do this
to depress or sadden us
but rather to gladden and encourage us.
When the church calls our attention to the cross,
it is to say to us:
there is no evil so dark and so deep,
so massive, so perverse, and so obscene—
not even the cross—
but that God can turn it into good.

The Worthy Mother of Your Son

Although reverence for Mary
goes back to the earliest times,
it was only when the staggering truth about Jesus
was more clearly understood and articulated—
   God from God, Light from Light,
   true God from true God—
                              (Creed)
that a lively devotion to Mary sprang up in earnest.
The thinking of the church seemed to be:
If Jesus is that great,
his mother, who gave him to the world,
must to a degree share in that greatness.

The connection between
the greatness of Jesus and the meaning of Mary
in the Catholic consciousness
is seen in the various titles used of Mary,
for example, the Ark of the Covenant.
The suggestion here is that
just as the presence of God in Old Testament times
was enshrined in the ark,
so God-in-Jesus was sheltered in the womb of Mary.
Mary has also been called
the Gateway of the Great King
to signify her role in making Christ present to us.
Through Mary, Christ passed
as through a gate to reach us.

One can understand that it is not by coincidence
that the great feast of Mary,
the feast of the Immaculate Conception,
occurs within the same month
as one of the great feasts of our Lord,
Christmas, the feast of his birth.
How wrongheaded it is to see devotion to Mary
as a sidetrack or even as a barrier
between a person and Jesus.
Devotion to Mary
is rather a smooth and easy access to him.

Through the Eyes of a Mother

For some curious reason, we human beings
find it more exciting to view things
through someone else's eyes rather than our own.
Novelists and storytellers have always understood this
and have sought to make us see life's situations
through the eyes of another.
The dynamic of the rosary works in just that way.
It makes us keenly aware of the mysteries
of Christ's life, death, and resurrection
through the filter of another person, namely, Mary.
We are meant to see and hear
and to emotionally react to these happenings
as Mary did.
The rosary is a classic example of a long-standing
Christian approach to Jesus through Mary.

Rising He Restored Our Life

Easter is a feast of life! What is life?
Some people see life as a rare privilege;
others think of life as a hideous curse.
Mark Twain, for instance, thought of it that way.
He once wrote of the human experience:

> The burden of pain, care, misery
> grows heavier year by year.
> At length ambition is dead.
> Longing for release is in their place.
> It comes at last.
> The only unpoisoned gift earth ever had for them
> and they vanish from a world
> where they were a mistake
> and a failure and a foolishness,
> where they left no sign that they ever existed—
> a world which will lament them a day
> and forget them forever.

(Source Unknown)

How bleak. How cynical and not at all the way
in which Christians view the matter.
For us Catholic Christians,
life is God's richest gift to people.
And this is why we make so much of Easter:
It celebrates abundance of life—
life that spills over from this world into the next.
As Christ rose to live again after his death,
so shall we.

Index